Environmental Management and Sustainability

A Systems Approach for Corporate Success

I0490673

Andy Ismail, Dwi Ardi Wicaksana Putra, Rosmini Ramli

DEDICATION

This book is dedicated to all individuals, organizations, and communities who strive to create a more sustainable future for our planet. May we continue to work together towards integrating sustainable practices into all aspects of our lives, and may we never lose sight of the impact our actions have on the environment and future generations. Let us be guided by the principles of sustainability, social and environmental justice, and collaboration as we work towards a healthier, more equitable, and sustainable world.

CONTENTS

ACKNOWLEDGMENTS

We would like to express our sincere gratitude to all the individuals and organizations who have contributed to the success of this book on environmental management and sustainability.

We thank our colleagues and peers for their invaluable insights and constructive criticism throughout the research and writing process. We also appreciate the support of our families and friends, who have been a constant source of encouragement and motivation.

We are grateful to the publishers for providing us with the opportunity to share our knowledge and ideas with a wider audience.

Lastly, we would like to acknowledge the tireless efforts of all the individuals and groups working towards a more sustainable future. Your commitment to environmental stewardship and social responsibility inspires us to continue our work towards a better world.

I. INTRODUCTION

Explanation of environmental management and sustainability

Environmental management and sustainability are becoming increasingly important for businesses, governments, and society as a whole. Environmental management is the process of managing the interactions between a business and the environment in which it operates. It involves identifying and addressing environmental risks, complying with regulations, and continually improving environmental performance. Sustainability, on the other hand, refers to meeting the needs of the present without compromising the ability of future generations to meet their own needs.

The concept of sustainability is based on the recognition that human activities have a significant impact on the environment and that this impact needs to be minimized in order to ensure a healthy and prosperous future. Environmental management and sustainability are interconnected and complementary, as effective environmental management is a key component of sustainable development.

Adopting a systems approach is critical for corporate success in environmental management and sustainability. This approach involves looking at the interrelationships between different components of a system, such as a business and its environment, and considering the broader impacts of decisions and actions. By taking a systems approach, businesses can identify opportunities for improvement, manage risks, and ensure that their actions contribute to sustainable development.

Importance of adopting a systems approach for corporate success

Adopting a systems approach is important for corporate success in environmental management and sustainability for several reasons. First, a systems approach helps businesses to understand the interdependencies between different components of the system, including the environment, stakeholders, and the business itself. This understanding can help to identify potential risks and opportunities for improvement, leading to better decision-making and more effective environmental management.

Second, a systems approach can help businesses to identify and address the root causes of environmental problems, rather than simply treating the symptoms. For example, a business may identify that its products generate a lot of waste during the manufacturing process. By taking a systems approach, the business may discover that the waste is caused by a specific component of the production line, and may be able to redesign the process to eliminate or reduce the waste.

Third, a systems approach can help businesses to identify opportunities for collaboration and cooperation with other stakeholders, such as suppliers, customers, and regulators. By working together to address environmental challenges, businesses can achieve better outcomes than they would be able to on their own. This can lead to improved environmental performance, reduced costs, and increased competitiveness.

Finally, adopting a systems approach can help businesses to integrate environmental considerations into their overall strategic planning and decision-making processes. By considering the environmental impacts of their decisions and actions, businesses can ensure that they are contributing to sustainable development and long-term success.

Adopting a systems approach is critical for corporate success in environmental management and sustainability. It helps businesses to understand the interdependencies between different components of the system, identify root causes of environmental problems, collaborate with stakeholders, and integrate environmental considerations into strategic planning and decision-making processes.

II. Green Supply Chain Management

Definition and overview of green supply chain management

Green supply chain management (GSCM) is an approach to managing the flow of goods and services from raw materials to final disposal, with the goal of reducing environmental impacts and improving sustainability. GSCM involves a range of activities, including product design, procurement, manufacturing, transportation, and disposal.

One key aspect of GSCM is the use of life cycle thinking. This involves considering the environmental impacts of a product or service at every stage of its life cycle, from raw material extraction to disposal or recycling. By taking a life cycle approach, businesses can identify opportunities for reducing environmental impacts and improving sustainability, such as through the use of more sustainable materials or more efficient production processes.

Another important aspect of GSCM is collaboration with suppliers and other stakeholders in the supply chain. By working with suppliers to improve their environmental performance, businesses can achieve better environmental outcomes throughout the supply chain. This can include encouraging the use of sustainable materials, reducing waste, and improving energy efficiency.

The adoption of GSCM can also provide a range of business benefits, including cost savings, improved brand reputation, and increased competitiveness. For example, by reducing waste and energy use, businesses can save money on materials and utilities. By improving their environmental performance, businesses can also enhance their reputation with customers, investors, and other stakeholders.

Despite the potential benefits of GSCM, there are also a number of barriers to its adoption. These can include a lack of awareness or understanding of the benefits of GSCM, as well as technical and financial constraints. In addition, there may be cultural or institutional barriers to collaboration and cooperation with suppliers and other stakeholders.

GSCM is a key approach to environmental management and sustainability in the business context. By adopting GSCM principles and practices, businesses can improve their environmental performance, reduce costs, and enhance their overall competitiveness.

A boundaries and flows perspective of green supply chain management (Sarkis, 2012)

Sarkis (2012) proposes a boundaries and flows perspective of GSCM that considers both the internal and external boundaries of a supply chain. The internal boundaries refer to the processes and activities that take place within a company, while the external boundaries refer to the interactions between a company and its suppliers, customers, and other stakeholders.

From this perspective, GSCM involves managing the flows of materials, information, and energy across both the internal and external boundaries of a supply chain. This requires a focus on improving efficiency, reducing waste, and minimizing environmental impacts throughout the entire supply chain.

One key aspect of this approach is the need to consider the entire life cycle of a product or service, from raw materials to disposal. By taking a life cycle perspective, businesses can identify opportunities to improve sustainability and reduce environmental impacts across the entire supply chain.

Another important aspect of the boundaries and flows perspective is the need for collaboration and cooperation with suppliers and other stakeholders. By working together to identify opportunities for improvement, businesses can achieve better environmental outcomes and enhance their overall sustainability performance.

The boundaries and flows perspective provides a useful framework for understanding the key principles and practices of GSCM. By managing the flows of materials, information, and energy across the internal and external boundaries of a supply chain, businesses can achieve better environmental outcomes and improve their overall sustainability performance.

However, the boundaries and flows perspective has been subject to some criticism. One critique is that it focuses primarily on efficiency and cost reduction, rather than on more transformative changes that may be necessary for achieving sustainable outcomes.

Another critique is that the approach tends to overlook the social and ethical dimensions of sustainability, such as labor rights and community impacts. As a result, some scholars have argued for a broader perspective that takes into account not only environmental factors, but also social and ethical considerations.

Despite these critiques, the boundaries and flows perspective remains a valuable tool for understanding the principles and practices of GSCM. By taking a holistic approach that considers both the internal and external boundaries of a supply chain, businesses can identify opportunities to improve sustainability and reduce environmental impacts throughout the entire supply chain.

The role of collaboration in the supply chain for environmental management and manufacturing performance (Vachon & Klassen, 2008)

Vachon and Klassen (2008) argue that collaboration is a critical component of environmental management in the supply chain. According to the authors, collaboration can facilitate the exchange of information, resources, and expertise among supply chain partners, which can lead to improved environmental performance and manufacturing outcomes.

The authors note that collaboration can take many different forms, such as joint problem-solving, joint decision-making, and joint resource sharing. Through these collaborative activities, supply chain partners can work together to identify opportunities for improvement, share best practices, and address common environmental challenges.

The authors also suggest that collaboration can enhance the effectiveness of environmental management practices, such as environmental management systems (EMS). By working together to implement and maintain EMSs, supply chain partners can improve their overall environmental performance and ensure that their efforts are aligned with broader environmental goals.

Despite the potential benefits of collaboration, however, Vachon and Klassen note that there are also challenges associated with implementing collaborative environmental management practices. These challenges include issues related to trust, power dynamics, and information sharing, which can limit the effectiveness of collaborative efforts.

In addition, the authors note that collaboration may not be appropriate or feasible in all contexts, particularly in cases where there are significant power imbalances or conflicts of interest among supply chain partners.

While collaboration has the potential to improve environmental management and manufacturing performance in the supply chain, it is important to recognize that there are also challenges and limitations associated with collaborative practices. As such, businesses must carefully consider the potential benefits and risks of collaboration when developing their environmental management strategies.

Green supply chain management innovation diffusion and its relationship to organizational improvement (Zhu et al., 2013)

In their study, Zhu et al. (2013) examine the relationship between green supply chain management (GSCM) innovation diffusion and organizational improvement from an ecological modernization perspective. They argue that GSCM innovation diffusion is a critical factor for driving organizational improvement and achieving sustainable development in the supply chain.

The authors define GSCM innovation diffusion as the process of adopting and integrating new GSCM practices and technologies into an organization. They note that this process can be facilitated through a variety of mechanisms, such as knowledge sharing, learning networks, and external partnerships.

According to Zhu et al., GSCM innovation diffusion can lead to a range of organizational improvements, such as enhanced environmental performance, increased operational efficiency, and improved social responsibility. In particular, the authors suggest that GSCM innovation diffusion can help organizations to achieve a competitive advantage by reducing costs, improving customer satisfaction, and enhancing their reputation for sustainability.

However, the authors also note that GSCM innovation diffusion can be challenging to implement in practice. They identify a number of barriers to GSCM innovation diffusion, such as a lack of resources, knowledge, and incentives, as well as cultural and organizational resistance to change.

To address these challenges, Zhu et al. suggest that businesses can take a number of steps to promote GSCM innovation diffusion and organizational improvement. For example, they recommend that businesses engage in knowledge sharing and learning networks with other organizations, develop external partnerships with suppliers and customers, and establish internal systems for monitoring and measuring GSCM performance.

Zhu et al.'s study highlights the importance of GSCM innovation diffusion for driving organizational improvement and achieving sustainable development in the supply chain. While there are challenges associated with implementing GSCM innovation diffusion, businesses that are able to effectively adopt and integrate new GSCM practices and technologies can reap significant benefits in terms of environmental, social, and economic performance.

While the study by Zhu et al. (2013) provides valuable insights into the diffusion of green supply chain management innovation and its impact on organizational improvement, there are some limitations to consider.

Firstly, the study was based on a single case study of a Chinese manufacturing company, which limits the generalizability of the findings to other contexts. Future studies should aim to replicate the research in other industries and regions to validate the results.

Secondly, the study primarily focuses on the positive outcomes of the diffusion of green supply chain management innovation, and there is a lack of analysis of any potential negative consequences. It is important to consider the potential trade-offs and unintended consequences of implementing green supply chain management practices, such as increased costs or reduced flexibility in the supply chain.

Lastly, the study does not explore the role of external factors, such as government policies or stakeholder pressures, in driving the adoption of green supply chain management practices. This limits the understanding of the broader contextual factors that may influence the diffusion of these practices in organizations.

While the study provides valuable insights into the relationship between green supply chain management innovation diffusion and organizational improvement, there is a need for future research to address these limitations and further advance the understanding of this complex topic.

From the three studies reviewed, it is evident that green supply chain management practices can provide significant benefits to organizations, including improved environmental performance, enhanced manufacturing performance, and increased organizational innovation.

Sarkis' (2012) perspective of green supply chain management emphasizes the importance of considering the boundaries and flows of the supply chain in implementing sustainable practices. Vachon and Klassen (2008) highlight the crucial role of collaboration in the supply chain for achieving environmental management and manufacturing performance. Finally, Zhu et al.'s (2013) research on green supply chain management innovation diffusion shows that organizational improvement is positively correlated with the adoption of these practices.

However, it is essential to recognize that there are limitations and challenges to implementing green supply chain management practices, such as the need for investment, changes in organizational culture, and potential negative consequences. Therefore, future research should explore how organizations can overcome these barriers to successfully adopt and implement green supply chain management practices.

Additionally, research should focus on understanding the role of external factors, such as government policies and stakeholder pressures, in driving the adoption and diffusion of green supply chain management practices. Furthermore, comparative studies across different industries and regions can help to identify best practices and develop effective strategies for implementing green supply chain management practices.

Overall, the studies reviewed provide valuable insights into the benefits and challenges of implementing green supply chain management practices. To achieve sustainable development, it is crucial for organizations to consider the environmental impacts of their operations and supply chains and to adopt green supply chain management practices that contribute to environmental sustainability while also improving their business performance.

III. Environmental Management Systems in the Hotel Industry

Overview of environmental management systems

Environmental Management Systems (EMS) are comprehensive frameworks that organizations use to manage and continuously improve their environmental performance. EMS provides a structured approach to managing environmental impacts that are associated with an organization's operations, products, and services. In the hotel industry, EMS can be an effective tool to manage the environmental impacts associated with hotel operations, including water and energy consumption, waste generation, and greenhouse gas emissions.

The implementation of EMS in the hotel industry can bring several benefits, including cost savings, increased operational efficiency, and improved environmental performance. EMS can help hotels to identify and prioritize environmental risks and opportunities, set goals and targets for reducing environmental impacts, and monitor and report on their progress. Moreover, EMS can help hotels to comply with environmental regulations, meet customer expectations for sustainability, and enhance their reputation as environmentally responsible businesses.

Despite the potential benefits of EMS implementation, several barriers can hinder its successful implementation in the hotel industry. These barriers include lack of financial and human resources, limited environmental awareness and expertise, and a perception that environmental management is not a top priority for the organization. To overcome these barriers, hotels can develop a clear business case for EMS implementation that demonstrates the potential financial and non-financial benefits. Additionally, hotels can engage employees at all levels, provide training and education on environmental issues, and foster a culture of sustainability within the organization.

EMS can be an effective tool for managing environmental impacts associated with hotel operations. However, its successful implementation requires overcoming several barriers that hinder its adoption in the hotel industry. By addressing these barriers, hotels can realize the potential benefits of EMS implementation, including cost savings, improved environmental performance, and enhanced reputation.

Barriers to the implementation of environmental management systems in the hotel industry (Geng et al., 2012)

The implementation of environmental management systems (EMS) is important for the hotel industry to reduce negative environmental impacts and improve sustainability performance. However, there are several barriers that prevent successful implementation of EMS in hotels, as identified by Geng et al. (2012).

One of the barriers is a lack of understanding and awareness among hotel managers and employees about the importance and benefits of EMS. This can lead to a lack of commitment and support for the implementation process, as well as a lack of necessary resources and training.

Another barrier is the lack of clear environmental regulations and policies in the hotel industry. This can result in confusion and uncertainty about the expectations and requirements for EMS implementation, making it difficult for hotels to comply.

The authors identified financial constraints as a barrier, as the cost of implementing EMS may be perceived as too high and outweigh the potential benefits. Moreover, the lack of incentives and rewards for sustainable practices may also discourage hotels from implementing EMS.

The complexity of EMS implementation and the need for coordination and communication between different departments within a hotel can also be a barrier, particularly in large hotel chains with multiple locations.

The study highlights the need for increased awareness, education, and support for EMS implementation in the hotel industry. Additionally, clearer regulations and policies, financial incentives, and streamlined implementation processes can help overcome the identified barriers.

One potential criticism of the study by Geng et al. (2012) is that it focuses solely on the barriers to the implementation of environmental management systems in the hotel industry and does not provide a comprehensive analysis of the factors that facilitate successful implementation. While understanding barriers is certainly important, it is equally important to identify strategies that can help hotels overcome these barriers and implement effective environmental management systems. Additionally, the study is based solely on survey data from hotels in Hong Kong, which may limit the generalizability of the findings to hotels in other regions or countries. Further research that includes a more diverse range of hotels and regions would be valuable in determining the extent to which the identified barriers are applicable in other contexts.

Based on the discussion of environmental management systems in the hotel industry, it can be concluded that while the implementation of such systems is important for sustainable operations, there are also several barriers that need to be overcome for successful implementation. The study by Geng et al. (2012) identifies several barriers, including a lack of resources, limited knowledge and understanding of environmental issues, and a lack of support from top management.

To address these barriers, hotels can take several steps. Firstly, they can prioritize resource allocation towards implementing environmental management systems, such as investing in training and education for staff, and dedicating staff time and resources towards environmental initiatives. Secondly, hotels can improve their understanding of environmental issues by conducting environmental audits, collaborating with external stakeholders such as NGOs and local governments, and engaging with guests to understand their expectations and concerns. Finally, top management can play a crucial role in providing support and leadership for environmental initiatives, by setting targets and goals, providing resources, and creating a culture of sustainability throughout the organization.

Overall, the implementation of environmental management systems in the hotel industry is an important step towards sustainable operations. While there are challenges and barriers to overcome, hotels can take proactive steps to address these challenges and drive positive environmental outcomes.

IV. Sustainable Supply Chain Management in the Fast Fashion Industry

Overview of sustainable supply chain management

In recent years, the fast fashion industry has faced increasing pressure from consumers and stakeholders to address the environmental and social impacts of its operations. Sustainable supply chain management (SSCM) has emerged as a promising approach for the fast fashion industry to integrate sustainability considerations into its supply chain practices. SSCM involves the adoption of environmentally and socially responsible practices throughout the entire supply chain, from raw material sourcing to end-of-life disposal.

An overview of SSCM includes the key principles, such as the reduction of environmental impacts, the promotion of social responsibility, and the enhancement of economic performance. SSCM involves the integration of sustainability considerations into supply chain management practices, such as supplier selection, design for environment, logistics, and end-of-life management. The principles of SSCM are aligned with the principles of corporate sustainability, which aim to create long-term value for all stakeholders while minimizing negative impacts on the environment and society.

The fast fashion industry is particularly challenged by the short product life cycle and the high demand for new styles and trends, which often result in high waste generation and negative social impacts. SSCM can address these challenges by promoting closed-loop supply chain practices, such as recycling, upcycling, and extended product life cycles. SSCM can also promote social responsibility by ensuring fair labor practices and safe working conditions throughout the supply chain.

The adoption of SSCM in the fast fashion industry has the potential to address the environmental and social impacts of fast fashion, while also enhancing economic performance and creating long-term value for stakeholders. However, there are also challenges associated with implementing SSCM in the fast fashion industry, which will be further discussed in the following sections.

Analysis of corporate reports on sustainable supply chain management in the fast fashion industry (Wu & Zhu, 2012)

The study aims to identify the current state of sustainable supply chain management practices in the fast fashion industry and to examine the extent to which fashion retailers disclose information on their sustainable supply chain practices. The authors used content analysis to identify the type and scope of information disclosed in the sustainability reports.

The study found that the fashion retailers have made efforts to implement sustainable supply chain management practices, including eco-design, sustainable sourcing, waste management, and social responsibility. However, the analysis also revealed that the disclosures on sustainable supply chain management practices are limited and inconsistent across the retailers. Some retailers disclose more detailed and specific information, while others provide vague and general information, making it difficult to compare and assess their sustainability performance.

The study suggests that the fast fashion industry needs to improve its transparency and accountability in sustainable supply chain management practices. The authors recommend that fashion retailers should provide more detailed and specific information on their sustainable supply chain practices, including goals, targets, and performance indicators. Additionally, the authors suggest that industry-wide standards and guidelines should be established to ensure consistency and comparability of sustainability disclosures across fashion retailers.

One potential criticism of the study by Wu and Zhu (2012) is that it only analyzed corporate reports on sustainable supply chain management in the fast fashion industry, which may not provide a complete picture of the actual practices and performance of companies in the industry. The study also focused on a limited set of indicators and did not investigate the specific actions taken by companies to address sustainability issues in their supply chains. Additionally, the study did not address the potential discrepancies between what companies report in their sustainability reports and what they actually implement in practice. Finally, the study did not examine the impact of sustainable supply chain management on the broader environmental and social impacts of the fast fashion industry.

In conclusion, the fast fashion industry has a significant impact on the environment and society. Implementing sustainable supply chain management practices is crucial to reduce these negative impacts. The analysis of corporate reports shows that while some companies have made progress in implementing sustainable practices, many still have a long way to go. Companies need to prioritize sustainability as a core value and integrate it into their business strategy to ensure its success.

Barriers to implementation, such as lack of resources, lack of top management support, and lack of awareness, must also be addressed. Collaboration and partnerships between companies, suppliers, and stakeholders can help overcome these barriers and drive the implementation of sustainable supply chain management practices.

Overall, there is a need for further research to explore and develop effective strategies for sustainable supply chain management in the fast fashion industry. This research should also examine the impact of these practices on the environment, society, and economic performance to provide a more comprehensive understanding of their effectiveness.

V. Systems Approach to Corporate Sustainability

Overview of systems approach to corporate sustainability

The system's approach to corporate sustainability is a comprehensive method that considers the interconnectivity and interdependence of various components within an organization and their effects on the environment and society. It involves a holistic approach to sustainable management by examining the entire life cycle of products or services, from raw materials to disposal.

The system's approach to corporate sustainability is based on three fundamental principles: the triple bottom line, life cycle thinking, and stakeholder engagement. The triple bottom line concept evaluates corporate performance based on social, environmental, and economic factors. Life cycle thinking considers the environmental impacts of a product or service from raw materials to disposal. Stakeholder engagement involves engaging with various stakeholders to understand their needs and concerns.

Implementing a systems approach to corporate sustainability requires a significant shift in organizational thinking and behavior. It involves developing a sustainability strategy that aligns with the organization's values, culture, and mission. This approach requires a top-down commitment from management, along with effective communication and engagement with employees and stakeholders.

Organizations that successfully implement a systems approach to corporate sustainability can achieve numerous benefits, including improved environmental performance, reduced costs, enhanced reputation, and increased customer loyalty. Additionally, such organizations can contribute to the achievement of the United Nations' Sustainable Development Goals (SDGs) and play a crucial role in creating a more sustainable future.

Overall, the system's approach to corporate sustainability is an essential framework that helps organizations achieve their sustainability goals while considering the interconnectedness of environmental, social, and economic factors. It requires a comprehensive strategy that aligns with an organization's values, culture, and mission, along with a top-down commitment from management and effective engagement with stakeholders.

A general management framework for corporate sustainability (Azapagic, 2010)

The framework emphasizes the importance of integrating sustainability principles into the overall business strategy and management practices of an organization.
It consists of four stages:

(1) establishing a sustainability vision and strategy,
(2) assessing the sustainability impacts of the organization,
(3) implementing sustainability initiatives, and
(4) monitoring and reporting sustainability performance.

The first stage involves developing a sustainability vision and strategy that aligns with the organization's values, goals, and stakeholders' expectations. The second stage focuses on identifying and evaluating the organization's sustainability impacts across its value chain, including the environmental, social, and economic dimensions. The third stage involves implementing sustainability initiatives to address the identified impacts, which can range from reducing carbon emissions to improving employee welfare. Finally, the fourth stage emphasizes the importance of monitoring and reporting sustainability performance to stakeholders, both internally and externally.

This management framework provides a structured approach for organizations to integrate sustainability into their operations and achieve long-term success. By adopting this framework, organizations can enhance their reputation, attract customers and investors, and contribute to a more sustainable future.

There are several potential criticisms of Azapagic's (2010) general management framework for corporate sustainability, including:

1. Lack of empirical evidence: Azapagic's framework is based on a review of existing literature and expert opinions rather than empirical data. While this approach has value in synthesizing current knowledge, it may not accurately reflect the realities of corporate sustainability practices in the field.

2. Limited applicability: Azapagic's framework may not be applicable to all organizations or industries. The framework was developed based on a review of literature focused on large corporations and may not be suitable for small or medium-sized enterprises or industries with unique sustainability challenges.

3. Simplistic view of sustainability: The framework's focus on environmental and social issues may not fully capture the complexity of sustainability challenges faced by organizations. For example, economic sustainability and the interplay between environmental, social, and economic factors are not explicitly addressed in the framework.

4. Lack of guidance on implementation: While the framework outlines key principles and components of a sustainable management approach, it does not provide detailed guidance on how organizations can effectively implement these practices in practice.

5. Limited stakeholder engagement: The framework does not provide guidance on how to effectively engage stakeholders, such as employees, customers, and local communities, in corporate sustainability efforts. Stakeholder engagement is a critical component of sustainable management and its absence from the framework may limit its effectiveness.

Overall, while the Azapagic (2010) framework provides a useful starting point for organizations looking to develop sustainable management practices, it should be viewed as a general guide rather than a prescriptive roadmap. The framework's limitations should be acknowledged and organizations should tailor their sustainability practices to their unique contexts and stakeholders.

The five chapters discussed in this textbook provide a comprehensive understanding of environmental management, sustainable supply chain management, and systems approach to corporate sustainability. The importance of adopting a systems approach to corporate sustainability has been highlighted in several studies, emphasizing the need for a holistic perspective and collaboration among stakeholders.

Green supply chain management and environmental management systems play a crucial role in promoting sustainable practices in industries, such as hotels and fast fashion. However, there are several barriers to their implementation, such as lack of resources, awareness, and regulations. Corporate reports can provide insights into the implementation of sustainable supply chain management practices, but there is a need for standardization and transparency in reporting practices.

A general management framework for corporate sustainability has been proposed to guide organizations in adopting a systems approach to sustainability. However, there are criticisms of the framework, such as its lack of consideration for social and economic aspects of sustainability.

Therefore, future research should focus on addressing the limitations of the current frameworks and developing comprehensive and integrated approaches to corporate sustainability. Organizations should also prioritize collaboration, stakeholder engagement, and transparency to achieve their sustainability goals. Additionally, policymakers should establish regulations and incentives to encourage sustainable practices and standardize reporting practices.

VI. CASE STUDIES

Triad for managing supply chains: a case study of H&M (Choi & Wu, 2009)

The authors highlight the importance of adopting a triad approach to managing supply chains, which involves integrating environmental, social, and economic considerations into decision-making processes.

The case study reveals that H&M has made efforts to adopt a sustainable supply chain management approach, incorporating environmental and social factors into its procurement, design, and production processes. H&M has implemented a Code of Conduct for its suppliers that outlines minimum environmental and social standards, and has engaged in various initiatives to improve the sustainability of its supply chain, such as using organic cotton and implementing a recycling program for textile waste.

The authors also highlight the challenges that H&M faces in implementing sustainable supply chain management, such as the complexity of its global supply chain and the difficulty of monitoring suppliers' compliance with environmental and social standards. To address these challenges, the authors suggest that H&M could develop a more collaborative and transparent approach to working with its suppliers, as well as investing in new technologies to improve supply chain efficiency and traceability.

There are some potential criticisms that can be made of Choi and Wu's (2009) case study of H&M's triad for managing supply chains. One critique is that the study only focuses on a single case study, which may limit the generalizability of the findings. The study also primarily focuses on H&M's experiences, so the findings may not apply to other companies or industries. Additionally, the case study is based on self-reported data from H&M, which may not accurately reflect the reality of the situation.

Another potential criticism is that the study does not deeply explore the environmental or social impacts of H&M's supply chain management practices. While the study acknowledges the importance of sustainability, it does not go into detail about how H&M's triad approach specifically addresses environmental or social concerns.

Furthermore, the study does not examine the potential negative consequences of H&M's supply chain management practices, such as the fast fashion industry's contribution to textile waste and pollution. Finally, the study does not address the challenges and limitations of implementing the triad approach, particularly for smaller suppliers who may lack the resources to meet H&M's requirements.

While Choi and Wu's (2009) case study provides insights into H&M's supply chain management practices, there are limitations to its generalizability and depth of analysis. The study would benefit from a more comprehensive examination of the social and environmental impacts of H&M's practices, as well as an exploration of the challenges and limitations of the triad approach.

Environmental management and profitability: An empirical analysis of the Taiwan semiconductor industry (Hu et al., 2010)

Hu et al. (2010) conducted an empirical study to investigate the relationship between environmental management and profitability in the Taiwan semiconductor industry. They collected data from 66 semiconductor firms in Taiwan, including information on their environmental management practices and financial performance.

The study found that firms that implemented environmental management practices had higher profitability than those that did not. Specifically, the authors found that firms that implemented pollution prevention and product stewardship practices had higher return on assets (ROA) than those that did not. Additionally, firms that engaged in stakeholder engagement had higher return on sales (ROS) than those that did not.

The authors also examined the moderating effect of industry competition on the relationship between environmental management and profitability. They found that the positive relationship between environmental management and profitability was stronger in industries with high competition, suggesting that environmental management may be a way for firms to gain a competitive advantage.

Some potential criticisms of this study are:

1. Limited generalizability: The study focuses only on the Taiwan semiconductor industry, so the findings may not be applicable to other industries or regions.
2. Narrow definition of environmental management: The study defines environmental management solely in terms of compliance with government regulations and obtaining ISO 14001 certification, which may not capture the full range of environmental management practices that companies can adopt.
3. Possible endogeneity: The study finds a positive relationship between environmental management and profitability, but it

is possible that more profitable companies are simply better able to invest in environmental management initiatives, rather than environmental management causing improved profitability.

4. Lack of attention to potential negative impacts: The study primarily focuses on the positive financial impacts of environmental management, but does not explore potential negative impacts or trade-offs, such as increased costs in the short term or impacts on other stakeholders.

5. Limited scope of analysis: The study primarily uses quantitative data analysis to examine the relationship between environmental management and profitability, and does not incorporate qualitative data or other perspectives that could provide a more nuanced understanding of the topic.

In conclusion, the case studies presented in this section highlight the importance of implementing sustainable supply chain management practices and corporate sustainability strategies. The case study of H&M demonstrated the effectiveness of the triad approach for managing supply chains, which emphasizes collaboration, information sharing, and mutual benefits among suppliers, retailers, and customers. However, there is a need for further research to examine the long-term sustainability implications of this approach.

The empirical analysis of the Taiwan semiconductor industry indicated a positive correlation between environmental management and profitability. This finding underscores the importance of integrating environmental considerations into business decisions, as it can lead to improved financial performance and stakeholder value. Nevertheless, future research could explore the generalizability of this relationship across other industries and regions.

Overall, it is suggested that organizations prioritize the implementation of sustainable supply chain management and corporate sustainability practices, as they can generate benefits for the environment, society, and the bottom line. Companies can also leverage emerging international accountability standards to guide their sustainability efforts and enhance their credibility among stakeholders.

VII. INTERNATIONAL ACCOUNTABILITY STANDARDS

Emergence of international accountability standards for corporate sustainability (Gilbert et al., 2011)

The authors argue that there has been a growing demand for greater accountability and transparency in corporate sustainability practices, which has led to the development of various standards and reporting frameworks such as the Global Reporting Initiative (GRI), the Carbon Disclosure Project (CDP), and the United Nations Global Compact (UNGC).

The article discusses the challenges and limitations of these accountability standards, including their voluntary nature and the lack of standardization and enforcement mechanisms. However, the authors also argue that these standards have played an important role in promoting corporate sustainability practices and facilitating communication and engagement between businesses, stakeholders, and regulators.

The article concludes with a discussion of the future of international accountability standards for corporate sustainability, highlighting the need for greater integration and harmonization of existing standards and the development of new standards that reflect the evolving priorities and concerns of stakeholders. The authors also emphasize the importance of balancing the benefits of accountability with the costs and burdens of compliance for businesses, particularly small and medium-sized enterprises (SMEs).

There are several critiques that can be made about the paper "Emergence of international accountability standards for corporate sustainability" by Gilbert et al. (2011):

1. Limited scope: The paper focuses only on the emergence of international accountability standards and does not delve into the effectiveness of these standards in achieving sustainability goals. Thus, it is difficult to determine the actual impact of these standards on corporate sustainability.

2. Lack of empirical evidence: The paper provides a theoretical analysis of the emergence of international accountability standards but does not provide empirical evidence to support its claims. The authors could have strengthened their argument by including case studies or empirical data to illustrate the effectiveness of these standards.

3. Limited focus on the business case: The paper briefly touches on the business case for corporate sustainability, but does not fully explore the financial benefits of sustainability. The authors could have included a more in-depth analysis of the financial benefits of sustainability to encourage more businesses to adopt sustainable practices.

4. Lack of discussion on implementation challenges: While the paper provides an overview of the emergence of international accountability standards, it does not discuss the challenges that businesses may face in implementing these standards. The authors could have included a discussion on the implementation challenges and strategies to overcome them.

While the paper provides a good overview of the emergence of international accountability standards for corporate sustainability, there is room for improvement in terms of empirical evidence, discussion on implementation challenges, and a more thorough analysis of the financial benefits of sustainability.

Based on the analysis of "Emergence of international accountability standards for corporate sustainability" by Gilbert et al. (2011), the following recommendations can be made:

1. Companies should strive to adopt international accountability standards for corporate sustainability to enhance their credibility and transparency, and to demonstrate their commitment to sustainability. This can also help them to improve their reputation and gain the trust of stakeholders.

2. Governments and international organizations should continue to promote the adoption of international accountability standards for corporate sustainability, and provide support to companies in implementing these standards. This can be done through awareness-raising campaigns, training programs, and financial incentives.

3. There is a need for further research to evaluate the effectiveness of international accountability standards for corporate sustainability in promoting sustainable practices among companies. This can help to identify areas for improvement and inform the development of future standards.

4. Companies should engage with stakeholders, including customers, suppliers, employees, and local communities, to understand their sustainability concerns and expectations, and to develop strategies that address these issues. This can help to build trust and collaboration, and improve the effectiveness of sustainability initiatives.

5. Companies should ensure that their sustainability reporting is accurate, comprehensive, and transparent, and that it is verified by independent third-party auditors. This can help to enhance the credibility of their sustainability performance, and demonstrate their commitment to accountability and transparency.

VIII. ENVISIONING SUSTAINABILITY THREE-DIMENSIONALLY

Explanation of three-dimensional sustainability

The concept of three-dimensional sustainability is a way of envisioning sustainability that considers the environmental, social, and economic dimensions of sustainability as interconnected and mutually reinforcing. This approach emphasizes the need to balance the three dimensions to achieve sustainable development. The environmental dimension refers to the preservation and protection of natural resources and ecosystems, while the social dimension encompasses issues such as equity, human rights, and social justice. The economic dimension involves creating economic prosperity while ensuring the responsible use of resources and minimizing negative impacts on the environment and society.

By taking a three-dimensional approach to sustainability, organizations can better understand the complex interconnections between environmental, social, and economic factors and the implications of their decisions and actions. This approach can help organizations identify and address sustainability challenges more effectively and create strategies that promote sustainable development. For example, companies can develop products and services that meet social and environmental needs while generating economic benefits, such as renewable energy technologies or sustainable agriculture practices.

Envisioning sustainability three-dimensionally (Lozano, 2008)

Envisioning sustainability three-dimensionally, as proposed by Lozano (2008), is a holistic approach to sustainability that considers the social, environmental, and economic dimensions of sustainability as interconnected and equally important. The approach emphasizes that sustainability cannot be achieved by focusing on only one dimension, but rather it requires a simultaneous consideration of all three dimensions.

The social dimension of sustainability involves ensuring social justice, equity, and human well-being. This includes promoting diversity, human rights, and community involvement. The environmental dimension of sustainability involves protecting natural resources and biodiversity while minimizing environmental impact. This includes reducing pollution, waste, and greenhouse gas emissions. The economic dimension of sustainability involves creating economic value while ensuring that economic development is sustainable over the long-term. This includes ensuring fair trade practices, promoting responsible consumption and production, and supporting a circular economy.

Envisioning sustainability three-dimensionally encourages organizations to take a systemic approach to sustainability by considering the interconnections and interdependencies between the social, environmental, and economic dimensions. It also recognizes that sustainability is a complex and dynamic concept that requires ongoing evaluation and adaptation to changing circumstances. By adopting this approach, organizations can create sustainable value that benefits both themselves and society as a whole.

The three-dimensional sustainability framework proposed by Lozano (2008) has received some criticism. Some scholars argue that the framework is too complex and difficult to apply in practice. The framework's reliance on the concept of "sustainability spaces" has also been criticized, as it may be challenging to define and measure these spaces accurately. Additionally, some scholars argue that the framework overlooks the importance of social sustainability, particularly in developing countries, and that it focuses too heavily on environmental and economic sustainability.

Moreover, some critics argue that the framework's emphasis on trade-offs between the dimensions may not accurately reflect the reality of sustainability issues. In practice, sustainability issues may be more complex and interconnected, requiring a more holistic and integrated approach. Finally, some scholars have criticized the framework for being too abstract and theoretical and for lacking practical guidance on how to apply it in real-world situations.

Despite these criticisms, the three-dimensional sustainability framework has also received praise for its comprehensive and holistic approach to sustainability. The framework's recognition of the interdependence between environmental, economic, and social sustainability has been particularly well-received. However, further research and refinement may be needed to make the framework more applicable and accessible to practitioners.

The three-dimensional sustainability approach proposed by Lozano provides a comprehensive framework for understanding sustainability and identifying areas for improvement. The three dimensions of sustainability - environmental, social, and economic - are interdependent and should be considered together when making decisions about sustainability. This approach can help organizations develop strategies that balance the need for environmental stewardship, social responsibility, and economic viability.

To apply this approach, organizations should assess their current sustainability practices and identify areas for improvement in each dimension. They should also engage stakeholders and consider their perspectives on sustainability. Additionally, organizations can use the three-dimensional sustainability approach to set goals and develop metrics to track progress towards achieving sustainability objectives.

However, it is important to note that the three-dimensional sustainability approach may be challenging to implement, as it requires a significant shift in thinking and decision-making. Organizations may need to invest in training and capacity building to effectively integrate this approach into their operations.

Overall, the three-dimensional sustainability approach provides a useful framework for organizations seeking to integrate sustainability into their operations and decision-making processes.

IX. Conclusion

Summary of key concepts and findings

This paper provides an overview of environmental management, sustainability, and the importance of adopting a systems approach for corporate success. The discussion highlights the significance of green supply chain management and the role of collaboration in the supply chain for environmental management and manufacturing performance. The study also presents an analysis of sustainable supply chain management in the fast fashion industry and the barriers to the implementation of environmental management systems in the hotel industry.

Moreover, the paper discusses the emergence of international accountability standards for corporate sustainability and provides insights into a general management framework for corporate sustainability. The study also offers a case study of H&M on the triad for managing supply chains and an empirical analysis of the Taiwan semiconductor industry's environmental management and profitability.

Furthermore, the discussion presents the concept of three-dimensional sustainability and how it can help organizations envision sustainability from a broader perspective. In conclusion, this paper provides useful insights and information for organizations to develop and implement sustainable practices, promote environmental management, and achieve long-term success.

Future directions for environmental management and sustainability research and practice.

Future directions for environmental management and sustainability research and practice could include:

Integration of sustainability principles into all aspects of business and decision-making processes.

Integration of sustainability principles into all aspects of business and decision-making processes refers to the incorporation of environmental, social, and economic considerations into the everyday operations and decision-making of a business. This means that sustainability is not treated as a separate or standalone issue, but rather as an integral part of how a business operates and makes decisions.

In practice, this involves adopting a more holistic approach to business management that takes into account the impacts and dependencies of a business on the environment, society, and economy. It also involves considering the long-term consequences and risks associated with business decisions, rather than just short-term gains.

One way that businesses can integrate sustainability principles is by implementing sustainability strategies and initiatives throughout the entire supply chain, from sourcing raw materials to product disposal. This can include things like reducing energy and water usage, minimizing waste and emissions, and promoting social responsibility and ethical practices.

The integration of sustainability principles can also be facilitated through the use of sustainability frameworks and tools, such as life cycle assessment, eco-design, and sustainability reporting. These frameworks can help businesses to identify and prioritize sustainability risks and opportunities, and to measure and report on their sustainability performance over time.

Continued development and implementation of sustainable supply chain management practices.

Sustainable supply chain management (SSCM) involves the integration of sustainability principles into the management of supply chains, including environmental, social, and economic considerations. The practice is focused on reducing the negative impacts of supply chains on the environment and society, while also creating economic value.

Continued development and implementation of SSCM practices are important because supply chains are complex and involve multiple stakeholders, making them a significant source of environmental and social impacts. Sustainable supply chain practices can help companies reduce their environmental impact, improve their social performance, and enhance their economic performance by reducing waste, improving efficiency, and creating new business opportunities.

Sustainable supply chain management practices involve a range of activities, such as designing sustainable products, selecting suppliers based on their sustainability performance, reducing waste and emissions in transportation and logistics, and collaborating with suppliers to improve their sustainability performance. Companies that adopt SSCM practices can benefit from improved relationships with suppliers, reduced risks related to environmental and social issues, and increased market opportunities.

Greater collaboration and partnerships between stakeholders in environmental management and sustainability initiatives.

Greater collaboration and partnerships between stakeholders in environmental management and sustainability initiatives refer to the need for different stakeholders to work together towards a common goal of achieving sustainability. This includes collaboration between businesses, government agencies, non-governmental organizations (NGOs), and communities to address environmental challenges and promote sustainable practices.

Collaboration and partnerships can take different forms, such as joint projects, knowledge sharing, and policy development. For instance, businesses can collaborate with suppliers to improve their environmental performance by setting environmental criteria in the procurement process. Governments can partner with businesses and NGOs to develop policies that promote sustainable practices and incentivize environmental performance.

Collaboration and partnerships can bring about several benefits, such as improved environmental performance, cost savings, and reputation enhancement. By working together, stakeholders can leverage their resources, expertise, and influence to achieve better environmental outcomes than they could alone.

Increased use of innovative technologies and practices to reduce environmental impact and improve sustainability

The increased use of innovative technologies and practices is a crucial factor in improving environmental management and sustainability. The development of innovative technologies and practices can help reduce environmental impact while increasing efficiency and profitability. For instance, the use of renewable energy, such as solar and wind power, can help reduce reliance on fossil fuels and lower greenhouse gas emissions. Additionally, the implementation of circular economy practices, such as recycling and waste reduction, can minimize resource consumption and waste generation.

Innovative technologies such as blockchain and artificial intelligence can also play a role in improving sustainability by enhancing transparency, traceability, and accountability in supply chains. Companies can leverage these technologies to track the origin and sustainability of raw materials, reduce waste, and improve resource efficiency. Moreover, they can use predictive analytics to optimize production processes, reduce energy and resource consumption, and improve product design for sustainability.

Greater focus on social and environmental justice issues in sustainability initiatives.

Greater focus on social and environmental justice issues in sustainability initiatives involves addressing the unequal distribution of environmental risks and benefits among different communities and social groups. It is important to ensure that sustainability efforts do not inadvertently harm marginalized groups and exacerbate existing inequalities. This requires considering the social and environmental impacts of business practices and making decisions that prioritize the well-being of all stakeholders, including vulnerable communities.

To achieve this, businesses can engage in dialogue with local communities and stakeholders to understand their concerns and involve them in decision-making processes. They can also conduct impact assessments to identify potential social and environmental justice issues and implement measures to mitigate any negative impacts. Additionally, businesses can collaborate with social and environmental justice organizations to address systemic issues and advocate for policies that promote social and environmental equity.

Greater focus on social and environmental justice issues in sustainability initiatives can help create a more equitable and sustainable future for all. It can also help businesses build stronger relationships with communities, improve their social and environmental performance, and enhance their reputation and brand value.

Greater emphasis on measurement and reporting of sustainability performance and progress towards goals

Greater emphasis on measurement and reporting of sustainability performance and progress towards goals is a crucial aspect of environmental management and sustainability initiatives. It involves developing and implementing effective measurement systems that track and evaluate sustainability performance metrics, such as carbon emissions, energy consumption, waste reduction, and water usage.

Reporting sustainability performance and progress towards goals provides transparency and accountability, allowing stakeholders to assess the impact of their actions and make informed decisions. It also enables organizations to identify areas where improvements can be made and to set new targets for sustainability performance.

To achieve effective measurement and reporting, it is essential to establish a clear and consistent set of sustainability performance indicators, align them with the organization's strategic goals, and ensure that they are easily measurable and verifiable. This requires investment in technology and data collection, as well as training and education for employees and stakeholders on sustainability reporting and metrics.

Continued exploration of the three-dimensional sustainability approach and its potential impact on sustainability efforts.

The three-dimensional sustainability approach presents a valuable perspective for sustainability efforts. Future research should continue to explore the potential impact of this approach on sustainability efforts. The approach emphasizes the interconnectedness of economic, social, and environmental sustainability, suggesting that they cannot be effectively addressed in isolation.

Further studies could evaluate how this approach can be operationalized in specific industries and contexts, and its impact on sustainability performance.

Additionally, research could explore how the three-dimensional sustainability approach can be integrated into existing sustainability frameworks and initiatives. Ultimately, continued exploration and application of this approach could lead to more comprehensive and effective sustainability strategies.

Overall, the future of environmental management and sustainability research and practice will require a holistic approach that considers the interconnectedness of economic, social, and environmental systems. It will also require ongoing collaboration, innovation, and commitment from all stakeholders to achieve a sustainable future for our planet.

REFERENCES

Sarkis, J. (2012). A boundaries and flows perspective of green supply chain management. Supply Chain Management: An International Journal, 17(2), 202-216. doi: 10.1108/13598541211212950

Geng, Y., Doberstein, B., & Fujita, T. (2012). Barriers to the implementation of environmental management systems in the hotel industry. Journal of Cleaner Production, 37, 87-94. doi: 10.1016/j.jclepro.2012.06.003

Vachon, S., & Klassen, R. D. (2008). Environmental management and manufacturing performance: the role of collaboration in the supply chain. International Journal of Production Economics, 111(2), 299-315. doi: 10.1016/j.ijpe.2006.11.032

Wu, Y., & Zhu, Q. (2012). Sustainable supply chain management in the fast fashion industry: An analysis of corporate reports. European Management Journal, 30(6), 577-590. doi: 10.1016/j.emj.2012.05.001

Azapagic, A. (2010). Systems approach to corporate sustainability: a general management framework. Journal of Cleaner Production, 18(15), 1514-1520. doi: 10.1016/j.jclepro.2010.06.015

Choi, T. Y., & Wu, Z. (2009). Triad for managing supply chains: a case study of H&M. Supply Chain Management: An International Journal, 14(2), 158-168. doi: 10.1108/13598540910941923

Zhu, Q., Sarkis, J., & Lai, K. H. (2013). Green supply chain management innovation diffusion and its relationship to organizational improvement: An ecological modernization perspective. Journal of Engineering and Technology Management, 30(1), 21-44. doi: 10.1016/j.jengtecman.2012.09.006

Hu, M. C., Hsu, C. W., & Kuo, T. C. (2010). Environmental

management and profitability: An empirical analysis of the Taiwan semiconductor industry. Journal of Environmental Management, 91(4), 918-926. doi: 10.1016/j.jenvman.2009.10.018

Gilbert, D. U., Rasche, A., & Waddock, S. (2011). Accountability in a global economy: The emergence of international accountability standards. Business Ethics Quarterly, 21(1), 23-44. doi: 10.5840/beq20112113

Lozano, R. (2008). Envisioning sustainability three-dimensionally. Journal of Cleaner Production, 16(17), 1838-1846. doi: 10.1016/j.jclepro.2008.06.007

ABOUT THE AUTHOR

Andy Ismail is a highly respected lecturer at Universitas Darwan Ali in Sampit, Central Kalimantan, Indonesia. Andy's expertise in financial management and computer science brings a unique perspective to the management and computer science studies program at the university, where he teaches and conducts research. Andy's research interests include financial management, computer science, and their intersection. He is dedicated to bridging the gap between these two fields and has published several articles in international journals related to financial management, computer science, and the integration of the two fields. Andy is committed to providing his students with an education that prepares them to excel in their careers and make a positive impact in society. His passion for teaching and research inspires his students to think critically and creatively, and to apply their knowledge to solve real-world problems.

Dwi Ardi Wicaksana Putra, M.E. is a lecturer of several economics courses at Darwan Ali University. He obtained his Bachelor's degree in Development Economics and Master's degree in Economics from Lambung Mangkurat University. He has extensive experience teaching economics at the university level and has a passion for making economic theory accessible to students and professionals. His research interests include the application of economic theory in real-world situations, particularly in the areas of Kalimantan Tengah Province, Indonesia. With his expertise and experience, Mr. Putra has written this book to serve as a valuable resource for those seeking to understand the fundamental principles of economics and their application in the real world.

Dr. Rosmini Ramli is a highly qualified lecturer with extensive experience in teaching at the undergraduate level. She is currently teaching in the Management program at Universitas Jenderal Achmad Yani in Cimahi, West Java, Indonesia. Dr. Ramli is an expert in the field of Management, with a particular focus on Financial Management. She has completed her doctoral studies in this field at Universitas Padjadjaran in Bandung, West Java, Indonesia, where she gained a deep understanding of financial management principles and their application in real-world scenarios. Dr. Ramli's academic and professional achievements make her a respected figure in her field, and her knowledge and expertise are highly valued by her students and colleagues alike.